CELEBRATING THE HOLIDAYS
WITH
TRAVIS AND MOLLIE

Written by Barbara Gay   Illustrated by Libby Nickel
Copyright 2017 by Just Fun Books & Things--4991 Manor Ridge Lane, San Diego CA 92130--All Rights Reserved.
Printed in the United States of America. No part of this publication may be reproduced or distributed in any form or by any means, or stored in a database or retrieval system, without the prior written permission of the publisher
ISBN 978-0-9990471-0-1 LCCN 2017904795

1

Travis, Mollie, and their family know that there are many different religious and other holidays in the world.

However, they don't celebrate all of those holidays.

Since they live in the United States, they follow the traditions and customs of their own family.

The World We Live In

JANUARY

There are TWO holidays in January—New Year's Day and Martin Luther King, Jr. Day.

Grandpa and Grandma always have a party on New Year's Eve, and Travis and Mollie get to stay up late and join the fun!

They try to get attention any way they can. They search for any food they may find on the floor.

Mollie's birthday is on Jan 3rd. She gets extra attention and a birthday cake!

They also celebrate Martin Luther King Day in January, but this is normally just a quiet day at home.

At the New Year's Eve party, Travis and Mollie enjoy seeing everyone and getting pats or nice words about what good dogs they are!

They are allowed to stay up late because they can sleep late the next morning.

FEBRUARY

There are also TWO holidays in this month! That means more family visits and more fun.

Valentine's Day is a special day for Travis and Mollie because they get to exchange valentine cards with their friends.

Grandma and Grandpa exchange cards also, and Grandma always gets flowers and candy.

The family also celebrates President's Day, but this is normally just a day to shop and play or to enjoy a quiet day at home.

Mollie thinks she is extra special on this day because Grandpa and Grandma sometimes call her Sweetheart instead of Mollie.

She thinks the holiday was named just for her!

MARCH

Travis and Mollie welcome St Patrick's Day in March by going shopping with Grandpa and Grandma to buy party supplies to decorate the house.

They especially enjoy going to parties and parades.

They love the extra attention they get when the parties are at their house!

They also enjoy seeing all of the green hats and costumes and listening to the Irish bands.

At home, Travis always gets in trouble because he likes to chew up the coins in the pot of gold that Grandma uses as a decoration.

Mollie sees Travis getting in trouble, so she doesn't try to get in the pot of gold!

APRIL

April has several holidays, but Easter is a favorite for both Travis and Mollie.

On Easter Sunday, they get to join in the Easter egg hunts with their family and friends.

They also enjoy seeing all of the grownups and children dressed up in their nicest clothes.

Travis's birthday is April 24th, and he gets extra attention and a birthday cake on his special day!

During this month, they also celebrate Passover and Earth Day with some of their friends and families.

Grandpa and Grandma help Travis and Mollie in their egg hunt by carrying their Easter baskets for them.

Travis and Mollie like to eat the eggs as soon as they find them! Grandpa and Grandma try to grab the eggs away from them before they eat too many!

MAY

There are TWO holidays in May--Mother's Day and Memorial Day.

On Mother's Day, Grandma always receives flowers or candy from Grandpa and everyone else in the family. Travis and Mollie enjoy looking at the beautiful flowers, but they are out of reach for them.

They still search the floor carefully in case someone drops a piece of candy! If they do, both dogs rush to see who can get to it first! Usually Mollie wins!

The whole family usually goes out to eat at a restaurant. Travis and Mollie stay home and enjoy resting after a fun day.

Mother's Day is a holiday for remembering all mothers. Memorial Day is a holiday for remembering all of our veterans and others who are no longer living.

Travis and Mollie enjoy one of the many parades.

JUNE

June has TWO very important holidays that both Travis and Mollie enjoy—Father's Day, and Flag Day.

On Father's Day, Grandpa receives gifts from everyone in the family! Grandpa also gets treated to a picnic. He normally barbeques a lot at home, but on this day everyone else cooks the food!

Travis and Mollie enjoy seeing all of the relatives that come to visit on this day. They also enjoy playing with their cousins and other doggie friends.

Flag Day is another holiday in June. The family always flies the flag, but they remember it more on this special day.

Travis and Mollie at a Picnic on Father's Day in June.

Travis looks for any food that may have dropped to the ground while Mollie enjoys looking at the people and scenery.

JULY

This month has one of the biggest holidays in the country—Independence Day or the 4th of July.

It is celebrated with parades in the daytime and fireworks in the evenings in most cities.

The only good thing about this holiday for Travis and Mollie is the family picnic.

They enjoy going to the parades, but they are scared and confused by the fireworks.

The noise from the fireworks hurts their ears.

Grandpa and Grandma try to comfort them by holding them and talking to them in soft voices to reassure them that they are safe and won't be harmed.

AUGUST

There are no official holidays in August, so Travis and Mollie make up their own!

They enjoy Dog Beach Days and Long Walk Days with Grandpa and Grandma. They also have Harbor Day when they sit on the pier and watch the boats sail by. Another favorite is Canyon Day when they look out the fence at activities going on in the canyon below. There is also Back-to-School Day. This is the day when all children return to school.

Travis and Mollie sometimes feel happy about Back-to-School Day because they enjoy the peace and quiet when the grandchildren are gone. At other times they feel lonely and miss having them around.

Travis and Mollie enjoy sitting on the pier on one of their own holidays.

Travis likes to watch the sailboats and fishing boats and Mollie likes to watch the rowboats .

SEPTEMBER

There are TWO holidays in September that Travis and Mollie celebrate with their family--Labor Day and Patriot's Day. They also celebrate Rosh Hashanah and Yom Kippur with some of their friends.

The family celebrates Labor Day at the home of Grandpa and Grandma's son. Everyone brings food, and they enjoy relaxing, talking, and swimming.

Mollie and Travis join in on the fun. Mollie likes to walk around the edge of the pool.

She has fallen in twice, so Grandpa and Grandma watch her closely!

The grandchildren are teaching Mollie to swim to the steps built into the wall of the pool so she can get out by herself.

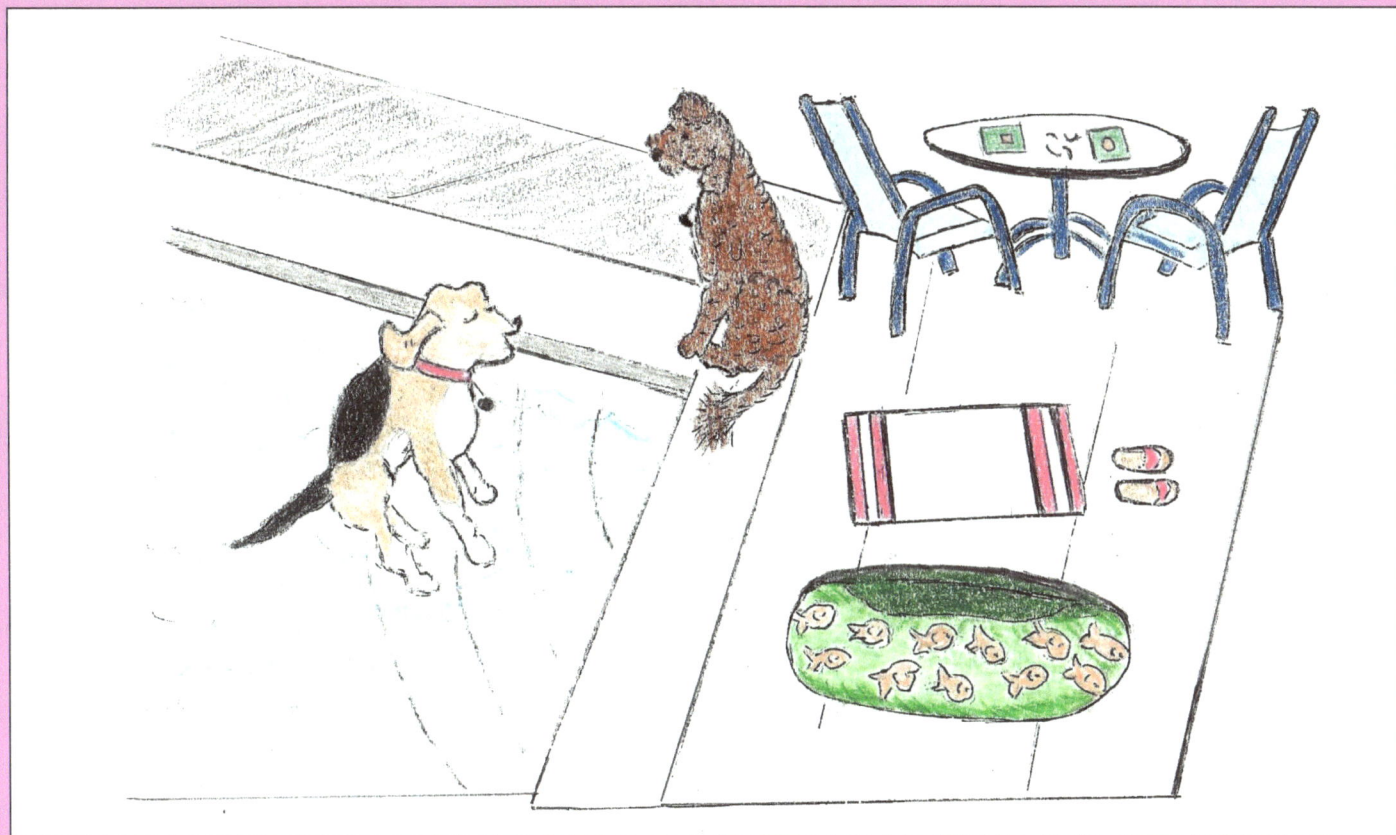

Travis stands next to the steps and watches her to be sure she gets out.

OCTOBER

There are TWO holidays the family celebrates in October—Columbus Day and Halloween.

Columbus Day marks the day Columbus discovered America. Travis and Mollie enjoy the day with friends and family as usual.

However, Halloween is one of their favorite holidays because they get to dress up in their costumes and go trick or treating with their family!

They know they can't have any of the candy because it isn't good for them, but they usually get doggie treats because everyone thinks they are cute!

Grandma always makes their costumes.

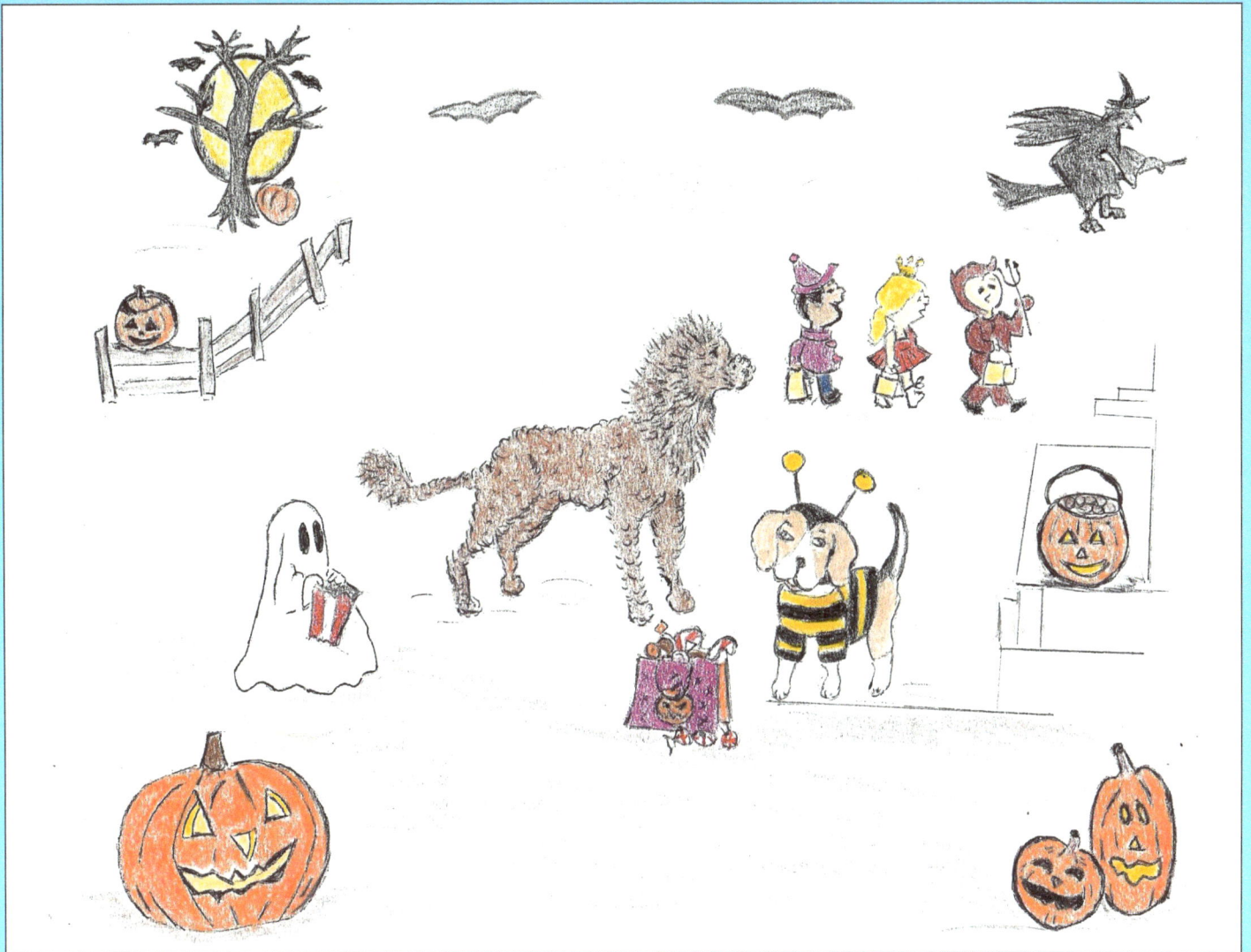

Travis usually goes as a lion and Mollie as a bumble bee.

NOVEMBER

There are THREE holidays in November: Thanksgiving Day, Veteran's Day, and Election Day.

Thanksgiving Day is "Feast Day" to Travis and Mollie! It seems to them that everyone eats all day long!

Election Day is a quiet day when all of the grownups go to vote.

Veteran's Day is a day for parades and to remember all of the men and women who are now serving or who have served our country in the armed services.

On Thanksgiving Day, there are plates of food on tables all over the house!

At meal time, the family enjoys turkey, dressing, and all of the other good things that go along with it.

DECEMBER

Christmas is the big holiday that Travis and Mollie celebrate with their family. They also celebrate Hanukkah with some of their friends and their families.

Travis and Mollie try to help their family put up a big Christmas tree, decorate it, and put presents under it. Everyone tells them they are just in the way!

When Christmas morning finally comes, the children and Travis and Mollie rush downstairs to see if Santa has filled their stockings and left presents for them.

They are not disappointed! They check their stockings and find lots of candy. Then they unwrap their presents and find many games, toys, and clothes!

December brings the year to a close. Right after Christmas, they get ready to start the next year and to enjoy more holidays with their friends and family.

For Marcus, Chiara, Sonja, Leilani and their children.

JUST FUN
Books & Things

Thanks to Ray, David, and Astrid for their patience and help to the writer while working on this book.

Thanks to Jeanette for her help with related products.

Thanks to all of the Humane Societies and other pet shelters who rescue, care for, and find good homes for all animals needing their help.

This book was inspired by the activities of Travis and Mollie--dogs who are owned, cared for, loved, and spoiled by the writer and her family.

Travis was bred by Tropico Kennels in Palmdale, CA. Mollie was adopted from the Rancho Coastal Humane Society in San Diego, CA.

www.ingramcontent.com/pod-product-compliance
Lightning Source LLC
LaVergne TN
LVHW072100070426
835508LV00002B/195